Well-Tempered Jazz

Piano Solos by Mark Hayes

Also available
Compact Disc • ND5008
Cassette • NC5053
Set of Parts for Guitar, Bass, Drums, Synthesizer and Percussion • LB5469

Cover Design by Terry Clouse

TABLE OF CONTENTS

FOREWORD

I am pleased to present the latest offering in the Well-Tempered Series from Shawnee Press, "Well-Tempered Jazz." Jazz is a truly American art form. From its roots in the slave songs of the Civil War era, it has evolved through the decades, encompassing everything from ragtime to big band, to rhythm and blues, to fusion, to the New Age sounds of the 80s and 90s.

Even though I have not formally studied jazz, I've always been attracted to the lush, complex harmonies and syncopated rhythms inherent in this musical genre. As a young pianist in the Church, any new sacred music which used jazz chords or rhythms immediately caught my ear. As I learned to improvise, I began to use jazz harmonies in place of traditional ones as I played and arranged gospel music. Those sounds have influenced me for over 25 years and have provided the foundation for my piano, choral, and orchestral writing.

As jazz has gained more acceptance and popularity in the Church, this project seemed like a natural next step for me. Although much of the important music of the Church is classical in nature and expresses beauty through solemnity and reverence, I believe jazz has a place in the Church as well because of its inherent spirit and spontaneity. How many of us have not felt our soul dance at the unrestrained passion of a good "jazz ride," or breathed that contented kind of sigh when we hear just the right progression of beautiful chords? When music causes us to smile or tap our feet, that's none other than the fruit of the Spirit, joy, welling up inside. I think jazz causes God to smile, too.

I have chosen hymns, spirituals, and gospel songs for this project that are appropriate for the jazz genre. There is a wide variety of styles from swing to pop, from Latin to New Age. For those of you who are church pianists, you may find that some of these arrangements can even be used in worship settings or church social functions. Whether it's for your own enjoyment or for a full-scale concert, I hope "Well-Tempered Jazz" provides a rich performing experience for you, one that refreshes your spirit, pleasures your ear, and causes all that listen to smile at least a few times. Enjoy!

Mark Hayes

Thank you to . . .

Corey Allen, for showing me the next level of jazz theory and harmony.

Lew Kirby, for saying yes to this project five years ago and having the patience with me to see it finally happen.

Terry Clouse, for exceptional design layout and cover art. Thanks, T, for your creativity and your friendship.

This book is dedicated to Hazel Burke, my first piano teacher, who taught me the rudiments of improvisation.

PERFORMANCE NOTES

One of the challenges of playing jazz is maintaining a steady tempo and playing "in the groove." As church pianists, we are not expected to play with rhythm sections very often. Consequently our ability to keep steady tempos or "swing" can be erratic at best. Rhythm parts for bass, drums, guitar, and synthesizer (where appropriate) are available so you can perform these arrangements like the recording. This can be a great chance for you to learn to play "in the groove," which simply means to play with rhythmic accuracy and to be in synch with the other players.

Any time I've notated "swing" or "jazz" in the tempo indication, eighth notes should be played with a triplet feel or loose dotted eighth/sixteenth note pattern. Some tunes like "Amazing Grace" have a bossa feel and should be played with even eighths. One common trap when playing syncopated rhythms is to rush or push ahead of the beat. Please guard against this. It is one thing that separates amateurs from professionals. You will also make a lot of points with your drummer if you don't rush! If you have problems playing any of the rhythms in the book, listen to the recording and imitate what I've done.

A word about chords might be appropriate here. Some of the chords I've chosen are quite complex and may be new to your ear. In some cases it may appear that I've altered every conceivable note in the chord without rhyme or reason. Please take an extra moment with those chords and make sure you are playing all the right accidentals. Chord symbols are indicated so you can check the written notes with letters or numbers in the chord symbol.

In jazz, it is very common to voice chords in an inversion other than the root position. Sometimes the tonic note is not even played. I've labeled chords by their most basic chord symbol, even though all the notes are not spelled out on the page. Oftentimes the bass note is played by the bass player and it would not sound good for the piano to double the bass line.

In the back of the book you will find an index of common chords. This is a resource for you to learn and understand more about harmony and chord symbols. Just as figured bass was the "shorthand" for Bach's day, chord symbols serve that purpose for us today. If you want to learn to improvise, it is crucial that you learn chords and their symbols.

I like to write large, expansive chords that often encompass an interval of a tenth or more. I realize that not everyone has large hands like I do, so I've tried to provide alternate voicings in those cases. If you see a tenth interval with no cue notes, try to play it as is, or roll it. All other extended reach chords will have cue notes that you can leave out if necessary.

I am primarily a "reader" and do not consider myself the best "ear" player. However, over the years I've developed my ability to improvise by looking at printed piano accompaniments and the chord symbols simultaneously and improvising from that. If you hear a chord you like in my arrangement, look at the chord symbol above and try to play that same chord in a different inversion and in another register of the piano. Once you've learned the original notes, experiment with playing those same chords and notes in new ways. That's the heart of improvisation. You don't have to make it up out of thin air.

When I recorded this project, most of the arrangements were written down note for note in advance. However when the other players joined me, I played less notes than what I originally wrote. In general, the more instruments you add to the mix, the fewer notes everyone should play. Guitarists and pianists play in similar registers and compete for aural space. Don't try to "fill" in the same places your guitarist does. Give him or her space to shine as well, unless you agree in advance to be the feature player.

These arrangements have been transcribed to stand alone as piano solos. In most cases they are exactly what I played on the recording, but occasionally I added or left out notes so the arrangement would make sense as a solo. If you play these with a rhythm section, you may want to play fewer notes, particularly in the left hand, since the bass player provides a tonal and rhythmic foundation.

Every Time I Feel the Spirit

This arrangement is a classic example of the old swing style popular in the 30s and 40s. The tempo should be quick, but played only at a tempo which you can swing comfortably. Notice all the rests in measures such as 5, 10, and 12. If you are not playing with a drummer, resist the temptation to rush though these measures. Rely on your internal metronome. This arrangement does not require much pedal and sounds best when played with the articulation I've indicated. Notice the different harmonies I've used to color the phrase, "Every time I feel the Spirit." Above all, play with spirit!

Redeemed, How I Love to Proclaim It

There's something elegant about a jazz waltz. Approach this setting with a lilting, unhurried style. Be careful to bring out the melody at measure 9. Notice that the arrangement moves from a steady swing feel to a free even-eighth note style at m. 81 and then back to the swing feel at m. 97. The triplet scale passages in ms. 64, 66, 103, 105, and 107 are easily rushed, so take a few moments to work out fingering so you can play them evenly and in tempo. I especially like the melody of the chorus, which provides a perfect opportunity to use a sequential V-I harmonic progression. If you've never read the words to this old hymn, take time to do it and you'll discover why this arrangement sounds so happy.

Amazing Grace

My first inclination was to set this hymn in a black gospel style. However I chose a more pop-bossa feel that was inspired partially by a recent trip I made to Brazil. By stretching the melody out and putting this song in 4/4 time instead of 3/4, it felt at home in a Latin groove. Because the melody is in a half-time rhythm, take extra care to make it "sing" above the accompaniment. It can easily be lost among all the other rhythmic components. Measure 68 needs some extra attention to get all the accidentals right. Don't rush through ms. 44, 80, and 116, even though there are just half-notes in these measures. At m. 89, I've purposely thinned out the rhythmic texture. Resist the temptation to add more notes or to rush through this section. The "groove" comes back around m. 101. Listening to the recording will help you make sense of this section.

Ms. 141-148 are your chance to improvise on the eight bar pattern. Since the melody stops at m. 117, the rest of the arrangement is basically a written-out improvisation on those eight measures. Review what I've done and imitate in the bossa style using those four chords until you're ready for the final ending.

Seasons of Life

The writer of Ecclesiastes says, "For everything there is a season, and a time for every matter under heaven." The older I get, the more I realize how cyclical life is. I see how patterns in life repeat and yet evolve, especially if you are willing to pay attention and grow. This original composition is based on an eight measure repetitive chord progression and melody that starts out rather simply and continues to evolve with additional layers and rhythmic complexity. This concept of theme and variations or ornamentation of a melody is a time-honored tradition. It is not unlike the simple bass line or "ground" in Pachelbel's *Canon in D*, which is repeated over and over with new layers of ornamentation, although "Seasons of Life" is decidedly more contemporary and pop in nature. This song ends like it begins, very simply and quietly, coming full circle, much like our experiences in life.

Feel free to play with the tempo in the first eight measures. If you're playing with a rhythm section you should lock in the tempo by m.9. At the bridge at m. 33, pay close attention to the articulation in the right hand. This section needs to have a bit more separation and punch than the first section. If you're feeling adventurous, try improvising a different melody during the two eight bar phrases at ms. 71-86 or repeating this section a few more times.

Just a Closer Walk with Thee

This beloved gospel song speaks of the "toils and snares" of this life, but also of the comfort of walking closely with Jesus. How ironic that our greatest comfort in life may occur when we're the most uncomfortable. I've set this tune in a quasi-blues style because blues have always spoken to that "hard" side of life. The easy, unhurried tempo and lush harmonies are meant to make the journey sweet.

If you are playing with a rhythm section, let the bassist play the lead-in on beats 3 and 4 of m. 16. Set a tempo which allows you to manage the technically demanding passages later in the arrangement. Even though this a swing feel, there are occasional sixteenth note passages which should be played evenly such as ms. 29, 31, and 32. From the third beat of m. 64 to the end of the piece should be played with even eighths as well. If the sextuplet groupings in ms. 39-40 seem a bit daunting, try playing a chord in the right hand incorporating some of the chord tones from the sextuplet. You could also chord through ms. 51 and 55 in lieu of playing the 32nd note passages.

Poor Wayfaring Stranger

This tune is one of my favorite spirituals because of its minor tonality. It lends itself to subtle dynamic shadings, interesting altered jazz scales, and complex harmonies. I like how it flirts with Bb major tonality in the chorus but inevitably comes back to the minor home base. Perhaps the bittersweet, major/minor quality of this song is underscoring the concept of being a stranger in this troubled land, but longing for the bright world to which we all hope to go.

Bring out the melody starting in m. 8 and keep the accompaniment figures in the proper balance with the melody throughout. The occasional grace notes that occur in the arrangement should be played as quickly as possible, sliding to the primary note, with emphasis on that note. As the arrangement grows in rhythmic intensity at m. 24, stay steady. That's a very easy place to rush. If you can't play the passage at m. 32 cleanly, you could play a whole note chord there, tied over from the previous measure, and let the drummer provide the motion for that measure. Notice the change in mood and articulation that occurs from ms. 39-53. As the energy peaks in ms. 78-81, stay steady, especially with all those syncopations.

His Eye Is on the Sparrow

When I recorded this song, I had the lights turned down low in the studio and I just improvised from a quickly sketched out lead sheet. By the second take, we had down on tape what was in my heart. I think this song is such a favorite and a comfort to people because of the hope and promise found in the text. I tried to capture in music the joy and faith expressed in the lyrics, "I sing because I'm happy. I sing because I'm free. For His eye is on the sparrow, and I know He watches me."

The beauty of this arrangement comes from its lush harmonies and uncluttered style. Take lots of time with phrases, exploring the nuances of each new chord and the subtle dynamic shadings you can achieve. Although the tempo is quite free throughout, the song naturally moves ahead at ms. 25 and 49. Please take extra time with m. 74 as you modulate to the key of Eb. Play this next section very delicately and "milk" those phrases!

Spring Comes Early

For those of us who grew up in the Midwest, the sounds and smells of a spring thunderstorm are a welcome experience after the harshness of winter. Sometimes as early as March, bulbs start sprouting up and it feels like spring is coming early. I've tried to capture that "new beginning" kind of a feeling in this composition. Listen for the peaceful sound of raindrops in the flowing piano part and how the initial motive changes gradually with each new eight bar pattern. Pay attention to the articulation starting at m. 25. If you are playing with other rhythm instruments, allow the bass player to improvise in a melodic style during the repeated section at ms. 104-105, while you provide the treble foundation.

This song is dedicated to a friend of mine, John Moriarty. He is the kind of guy who lights up a room when he walks in. After struggling with alcohol addiction for several years, he is on the road to recovery. It is as if he is now fully alive for the first time in his life. The creative energy, love, and presence he brings to the table is much like the first spring rain, which washes away the cold of winter, and brings promise of new life once again.

Precious Lord, Take My Hand

This song was written in the 1930s and popularized by Tommy Dorsey, of big band fame. The simple 16 bar melody, which serves as both verse and chorus, was a perfect vehicle to showcase the smooth, mellow sounds of Dorsey's trombone. I like the sincere, earnest expression of the lyrics, "Hear my cry, hear my call, hold my hand, lest I fall." We've all been there and counted on that hand to guide up home.

The first verse should be played very freely with an even eighth note feel. Set a slow, steady tempo at m. 15 that allows you to play the intricate sixteenth note passages cleanly and evenly. Keep the energy building from the middle of the second verse at m. 45 throughout the third verse. Let it really swing! Play with abandon!

Old Time Religion/Swing Low, Sweet Chariot

I've arranged both of these songs chorally, but never for just piano. Although "Swing Low, Sweet Chariot" is traditionally heard in a slow, free-flowing style, I thought it would be creative to "swing it" at a faster tempo alternating with "Old Time Religion." Hopefully the result is a joyous rendition of two favorite old spirituals. If playing with a rhythm section, the bass player should enter at m. 13, allowing, the pianist to set the feel with the walking bass line in the first 12 bars. Give special care to the staccato articulation throughout and try accenting different notes in the melody, especially ones on the off beats. In m. 24, try sliding off the grace notes into the third intervals. Play it a little "carelessly." If playing with a bassist, don't double the left hand in m. 28. Let it be a bass solo. Continue to drive the energy through ms. 60-68, setting up the splashy modulation. If playing without a drummer, you'll have to feel the ritard by yourself. Listening to the recording will help you get the feel of it. As you pull back the tempo for one last chorus, sustain the energy all the way to m. 81. Play the Count Basie ending suddenly softer and give that last Bb 13 (#11) chord a good raucous tremolo and stinger!

Every Time I Feel The Spirit

TRADITIONAL SPIRITUAL

Arranged by
MARK HAYES (ASCAP)

Redeemed, How I Love To Proclaim It

Words by
FANNY J. CROSBY (1820-1915)

Music by
WILLIAM J. KIRKPATRICK (1838-1921)

Arranged by
MARK HAYES (ASCAP)

Amazing Grace

Words by
JOHN NEWTON (1725-1807)

VIRGINIA HARMONY, 1831

Arranged by
MARK HAYES (ASCAP)

Copyright © 1998, GlorySound
A Division of Shawnee Press, Inc.
International Copyright Secured   All Rights Reserved
SOLE SELLING AGENT: SHAWNEE PRESS, INC., DELAWARE WATER GAP, PA 18327

HE5044

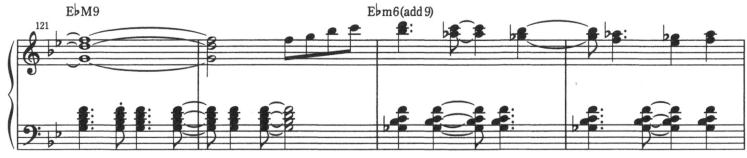

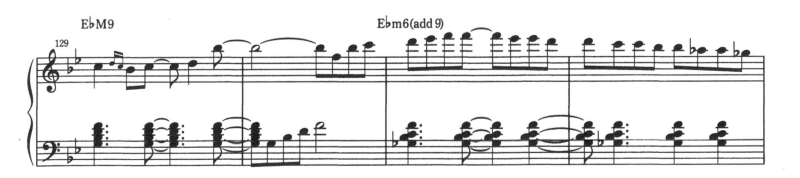

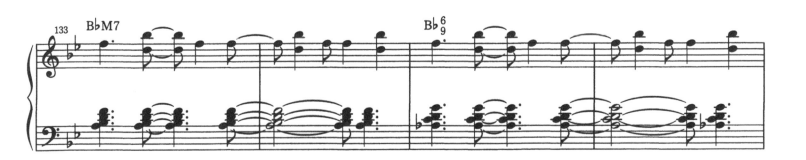

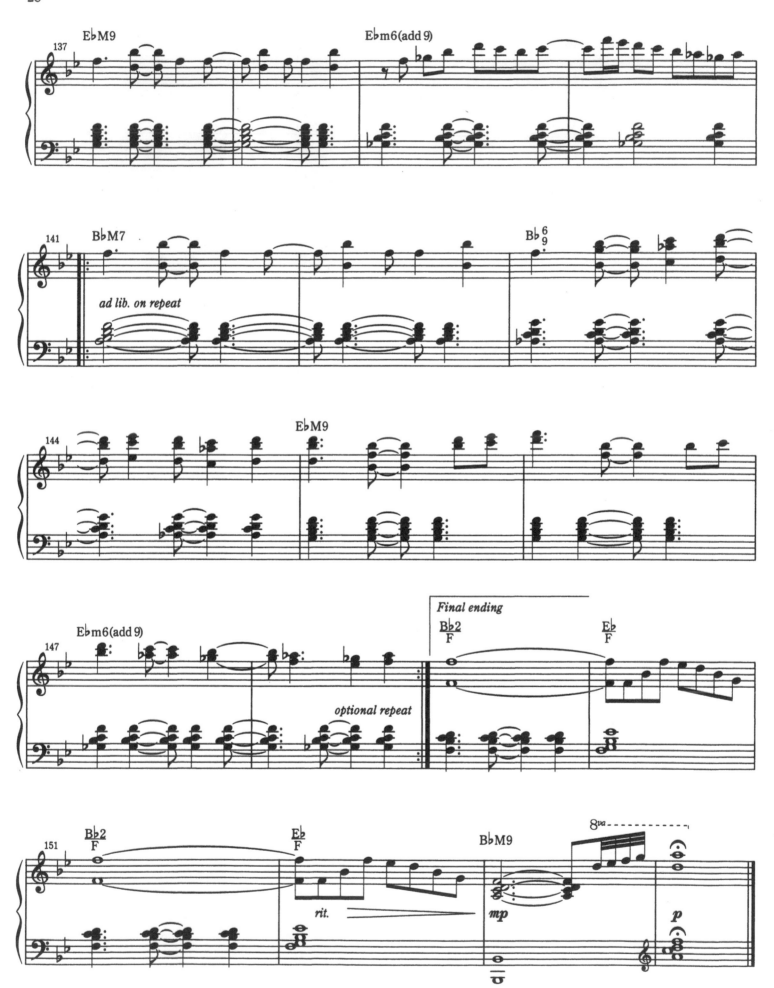

Seasons of Life

Music by
MARK HAYES (ASCAP)

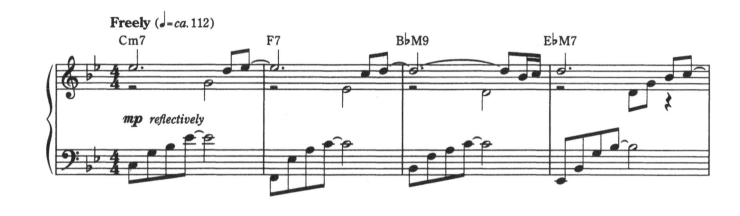

Just A Closer Walk With Thee

COMPOSER UNKNOWN

Arranged by
MARK HAYES (ASCAP)

Poor Wayfaring Stranger

TRADITIONAL SPIRITUAL

Arranged by
MARK HAYES (ASCAP)

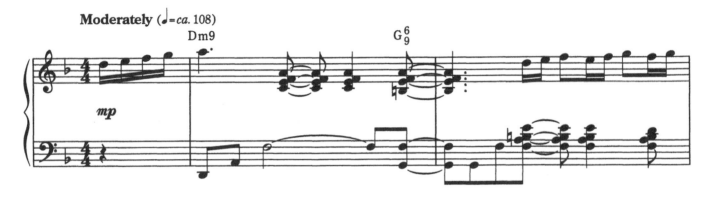

43

HE5044

His Eye Is On The Sparrow

Words by
CIVILLA D. MARTIN (1869-1948)

Music by
CHARLES H. GABRIEL (1856-1932)

Arranged by
MARK HAYES (ASCAP)

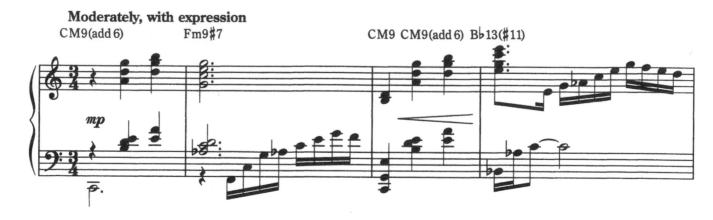

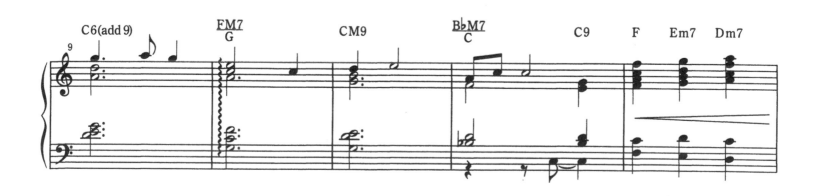

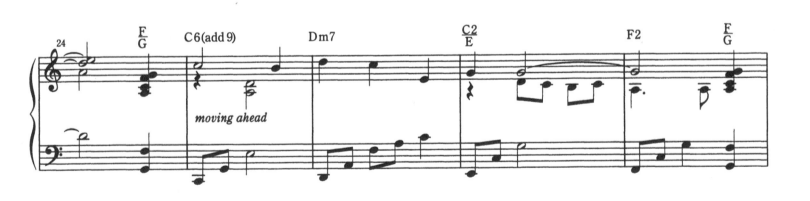

for John

Spring Comes Early

Music by
MARK HAYES (ASCAP)

Precious Lord, Take My Hand

Music by GEORGE N. ALLEN

Arranged by MARK HAYES (ASCAP)

64

Old-Time Religion
with
Swing Low, Sweet Chariot

TRADITIONAL SPIRITUALS

Arranged by
MARK HAYES (ASCAP)

Common Chords

Chords can be named in more than one way. These are some of the standard chord symbols used in church and popular music.

Also available from Mark Hayes...

the first four volumes in the Well-Tempered Series

Well-Tempered Praise

the first book in this bestselling series contains the following:

Pass It On; What Child Is This?; Nobody Knows the Trouble I've Seen/All Day, All Night; Interlude; It Is Well with My Soul; Carol Medley (Good Christian Men, Rejoice; Bring a Torch, Jeannette, Isabella; It Came upon the Midnight Clear; Angels We Have Heard on High); The Love of Jesus Medley (Jesus Love Me; I Love You with the Love of the Lord; Oh, How He Loves You and Me); Once to Every Man and Nation; The Church's One Foundation

Book .... HE5030   Listening Cassette NC5022
Book/Listening Cassette Combination GN5017

Well-Tempered Praise II

More excellent writing for piano... useful for services and concerts:

Praise to the Lord, the Almighty; He Giveth More Grace/No One Ever Cared for Me Like Jesus; Neo-Classique; Higher Ground; Sing Hallelujah; Alfred Burt Carol Medley (Caroling, Caroling; The Star Carol; Some Children See Him; Come, Dear Children); How Majestic Is Your Name; Silent Night; Jesus, Keep Me Near the Cross; Resurrection Medley (Low, In the Grave He Lay!; Christ the Lord Is Ris'n Today; Rise Again).

Book .... HE5032   Listening Cassette NC5032
Book/Listening Cassette Combination GN5027

Well-Tempered Praise III

Continuing the tradition of fine piano music:

Sing to the Lord (the Sandi Patti hit); The Light of the World Is Jesus; Simple Gifts; I Need Thee Every Hour; Shall We Gather at the River/Near to the Heart of God; For unto Us a Child Is Born; Joysong; Joshua Fit the Battle of Jericho; People Need the Lord; Praise His Greatness (HYFRYDOL; Great Is the Lord).

Book .... HE5034   Listening Cassette NC5034
Book/Listening Cassette Combination GN5042

Well-Tempered Christmas

Well-Tempered for the Christmas season:

Joy to the World; Sing We Now of Christmas; Rise up, Shepherds, and Follow; O Little Town of Bethlehem; O Come, All Ye Faithful; Holiday Medley (Jingle Bells, Deck the Halls, The Twelve Days of Christmas, We Wish You A Merry Christmas); We Three Kings; Manger Medley (Infant Holy, Infant Lowly; Away in a Manger); I Wonder As I Wander; Masters in This Hall

Book .... HE5038   Listening Cassette NC5046
Listening CD .... ND5002   Book/Listening Cassette Combination GN5051
Book/Listening CD Combination GN5052